# TRAINING YOUR DOG

The need to train a dog, for whatever purpose it may be kept, to conform to a certain code of behaviour both indoors and out, is becoming more and more widely recognised by dog lovers everywhere. Here is a book written in non-technical language especially for the ordinary dog owner which will enable anyone successfully to train a dog of any breed. In it will be found simple straightforward instructions indicating how to teach a dog all that is necessary to ensure its being a delightful and reliable companion - a social asset instead of a nuisance or an embarrassment.

*General Editor:* CHRISTINA FOYLE

*Foyles Handbooks for dog lovers*

---

*In Preparation*

# TRAINING
# YOUR DOG

*by*

*E. FITCH DAGLISH*

FOYLES HANDBOOKS
LONDON

© W. & G. Foyle Ltd. 1963

First published 1963
Reprinted 1964
Reprinted 1968
Reprinted 1970
Reprinted 1972
Reprinted 1975
Reprinted 1976
Reprinted 1979

Published in Great Britain by
W. & G. Foyle Ltd.,
125 Charing Cross Road,
London WC2H 0EB

Printed and bound in Great Britain
at The Pitman Press, Bath

# CONTENTS

# ILLUSTRATIONS

## Acknowledgment

*All the dogs shown in the illustrations are Rottweilers. The photographs in which they feature were taken specially for this book by Mrs. Mary Macphail and other members of the Rottweiler Club to whom I am deeply indebted.*     *E. F. D.*

# CHAPTER ONE

# BASIC PRINCIPLES OF TRAINING

IN THE modern world owning a dog may be a blessing or a curse. Whether it is the one or the other depends very largely on whether or not the dog has been trained to become part of the social structure of the community in which he lives. The necessity of training a dog to conform to a certain code of behaviour in whatever circumstances he may live is becoming more and more widely recognised by dog lovers both in town and country areas. Today one hears a good deal about training dogs for special duties, with the police, for guidance of the blind, for guards with the Royal Air Force and Army and other purposes, and of the training classes which are held up and down the country to help with advanced training. Opinions may vary as to the desirability of submitting a dog valued solely as a pet or companion to training of this kind, but everyone who owns a dog must wish him to be clean in the house, obedient in the sense that he will come when called, walk freely and comfortably on a lead and be under proper control when given his freedom in a park or the open country, and generally be a safe, reliable and thoroughly satisfactory companion to his owner or members of the family whose home he shares. The owner of a dog accepts responsibility for his good behaviour with humans, both adults and children, with farm stock of all kinds and with street traffic. A dog which is badly behaved, because untrained, may wreak havoc in the streets, in the fields or even in the home, and cause his owner to be heavily mulcted for damages.

Another important point is that a trained dog is very much happier than one which is left untrained. Without some sort of training there can be no real understanding between a dog and his owner. The aim of this handbook is to indicate how a dog wanted to fill the role of household or family companion may be taught the things which every owner wishes it to know and which will ensure its behaving in such a manner as to make it a social asset instead of an embarrassment. The more advanced or specialised types of training are not dealt with, as they are likely to be beyond the powers of the ordinary owner to tackle successfully. A reader who, having trained his dog in the simple exercises dealt with in the following pages, desires to go on to more advanced work, is advised to join a local Obedience Training Class and put himself and his dog in the hands of the specialist instructor.

Before proceeding to explain the methods of teaching the various exercises, it is necessary to say something regarding the mind of the dog, its limitations and how it works. Perhaps the most important principle to grasp at the outset of training is that a dog is not gifted with human intelligence, and has no sense of morals as we understand the word. A dog is unable to reason. He can learn only by the association of ideas. A devoted owner will often claim that his dog understands every word that is said to him. That is never true. In fact, a dog is quite unable to understand any words at all. If he appears to do so it is because he has come to associate a particular sound with a certain movement or course of action. In the same way he will learn to associate a particular experience, whether pleasant or unpleasant, with a certain sound or visual expression, such as a hand signal. Thus, your dog may be taught to take up a sitting position on the command SIT, but it would be equally easy to train him to assume the same posture by using the word Stand or Run, or by uttering any other sound, vocal or non-vocal. It is, therefore, most important to make use of the minimum number of words and to be sure always to use the same word for the same command. Be careful, too, that all commands are given clearly and incisively.

Never under or over estimate your dog's intelligence. By nature a dog is neither stupid nor wilfully disobedient. Start off with the assumption that your dog wants to please you, and never forget that successful training must be based on mutual confidence and affection. A dog's memory is retentive and his intelligence limited. He cannot be expected to adapt his behaviour to the changing moods of his owner. Strive, therefore, to be consistent in your training and be ever on the alert to refrain from teaching your dog to act in a way which may cause annoyance at some future time. For example, it may seem fun to teach a puppy to tug and bite at some object held in your hand and if, in the excitement of the game, he starts to bark and snap, to consider his behaviour amusing. But as he grows, this sort of game may lead to his becoming rough and destructive, if not actually vicious, and it may take much time and trouble to break him of a habit which you originally encouraged.

Never scold or punish a dog for doing something, or for failing to carry out a command, unless you are quite sure he knows just what is required of him and that he understands for what he is being punished. Don't be too ready to assume that he knows what you want him to do. If he fails to behave in the way you intend, it may be either that he has not understood the significance of your command or has not yet formed a sufficiently clear association between your order and the action it is intended to induce. Don't shout at your dog and never lose your temper, however exasperating he may seem to be. In all forms of training kindness and patience are essential if success is to be achieved. Dogs differ as regards the ease with which they can be taught to respond to the commands of their trainers. Some breeds are much quicker at learning certain exercises than others, as are some individuals, but the earlier in life training is commenced the better. But, though a youngster will learn more readily than an older adult, almost any dog may be taught all the exercises described in the following chapters by a trainer who is understanding and patient. No dog is ever too old to learn.

A dog trained by kindness, coupled when necessary with

firmness, will not only be more reliable in obeying commands than one which has been bullied into submission, but will also show by his general demeanour that he thoroughly enjoys doing the things he has been taught to do. If you teach your dog to obey commands uttered quietly you will, in an emergency, be able, by raising your voice, to attract his attention when he shows signs of succumbing to a sudden temptation to ignore his previous training; whereas if all commands are given in a loud, shouting tone he will become so accustomed to that tone that you may be powerless to arrest his attention when he wants to be off. The tone of voice used is of great importance in any kind of training. As already mentioned, a dog does not understand the meaning of actual words. He acts in accordance with the association a particular sound conjures up in his mind, and the tone of voice in which that sound is uttered will convey much more to him than the word itself.

One of the basic principles of training is to get a dog to associate the carrying out of commands with pleasure, and failure to act in the way indicated by his owner with discomfort. That is another way of saying that we reward him for doing something of which we approve and correct or punish him for doing something of which we do not approve. All training depends on applying suitable reward or correction at the right time and to varying them, to some extent, according to the understanding and temperament of the individual animal under training. This last point needs careful attention. What may be mild correction in the case of a robust, self-willed and boisterous dog, might be much too severe a punishment for a shy, timid or very sensitive pupil. The object of rewarding a dog after he has done what he has been told to do is to give him pleasure, and thereby to build up in his mind the association of the act with a pleasant experience. What form the reward takes is immaterial.

In the early stages of training the use of morsels of food or tit-bits may be convenient, but this must not be overdone later on. A dog which does as he is told because he hopes thereby to get a piece of biscuit, cake or meat, is not obedient in the best sense. As soon as a feeling of attachment or affection has been built up as between owner and dog, a friendly pat or words of praise will be appreciated as much as a tit-bit and will be sufficient reward for compliance with a command. But always make use of the same words or phrase when praising your dog, so that he comes to associate those words and the tone in which you utter them with being praised, and thus rewarded, for having pleased you. If when fussing or making much of your dog you use the term 'Good Boy' or 'Clever Chap', reserve those expressions for that particular purpose and don't make use of them at times when they can have no real meaning. If you do they will cease to have any significance when used to reward good behaviour.

Don't make training lessons unduly long, especially when dealing with a puppy or a dog which is in the early stages of being trained. As soon as signs of flagging attention, boredom or resentment are noticed suspend the session. A dog which seems to be stupid or stubborn may be merely tired or hungry, and if he obeys commands at all will do so unwillingly or with an air of dejection. Never miss an opportunity of rewarding your dog, even when he makes an effort to do as you command without much success. Throughout training be lavish with praise and very sparing of punishment. Never strike or smack a puppy and never use a stick or other weapon on any dog. If you do, you will probably forfeit his confidence and respect. A sensitive animal may be cowed and spoiled in temperament, while a bolder or more assertive one will probably retaliate or become resentful, unreliable or vicious.

Finally, try by every means in your power to make your dog regard training sessions as a game, but be sure that it is a game of which you never lose control and which can be stopped at any time at your discretion. Almost any dog will perform some exercises more readily than others and, by keeping close watch on your dog's reactions and behaviour during lessons, you will be able to see which details of training he finds most irksome. Do not try to overcome his unwillingness to perform the actions he dislikes by unsympathetic coercion or force. Rather reduce the time spent on the exercise during a session and encourage him by speaking to him in a friendly or jocular tone; and be sure to reward him generously whenever he acts, or tries to act, in the way desired. If patience and encouragement are practised by the trainer in such cases success will eventually be achieved.

# CHAPTER TWO

# YOUR NEW PUPPY

M OST people acquire a puppy when it is about eight weeks of age, and the first problem which has to be faced is how to get it to settle down comfortably, and behave reasonably well, in its new surroundings. Even at this early age the youngster is quite intelligent enough to absorb the rudiments of training which will help it to grow up into the obedient and delightful companion every dog owner wishes to possess. In a puppy mental activity begins before it leaves its dam. From the age of about three weeks it will register impressions received from the outside world, and while still very young its attitude towards the conditions in which it is to live later is formed; so that its treatment as a baby may have a permanent effect on its basic temperament.

Intelligence develops very quickly in a puppy. By the time it is three months old it is capable of learning almost everything that can be taught to a dog of any age, though, of course, its undeveloped body will be much too immature to permit it to respond physically to certain types of training. But while this indicates the importance of beginning training as early as possible, one must realise that an eight weeks' old dog is still a baby, with little or no understanding of the need to adapt its behaviour to unfamiliar conditions, and with no experience of life away from the protection of its dam and the companionship of its litter brothers and sisters. When first introduced to its new home it will probably be upset by the noise and bustle experienced during its journey from its previous home and be shy and bemused by unaccustomed sights and sounds. Even the unfamiliar scent and voice of its new owner may add to its bewilderment. A well reared puppy is, however, naturally sociable and if given time to get used to its strange environment will soon delight in being petted, talked to and admired by anyone who greets it with friendly words and gestures. The first necessity is to give it confidence; to make it understand that the new world in which it finds itself holds no menace – that its safety and independence is not threatened.

If at first it seems very timid and hides behind the furniture, on no account try to drag it from its hiding place by force, or worry it by too much attention. Either leave it until it emerges of its own free will or approach it quietly and pick it up gently, making all your movements slow and soothing. Never try to grab a puppy, or pick it up by the scruff of the neck. When lifting it place one hand under its quarters and the other beneath the chest. This will tend to quieten it, especially if it is spoken to in a soothing tone, and will hold it safely even should it struggle to get free.

When dealing with a young puppy every effort must be made to gain its confidence. Try to get it to associate coming to you with pleasure and security. If at first it seems shy, do not make the mistake of moving towards it. This will probably only add to its fear and cause it to run away and hide. Instead, try to coax it to come to you. You may do this by offering it a tit-bit or holding out your hand and letting the youngster smell and lick it. Do not be in a hurry. The ideal is to let the puppy come to you by its own volition, and when it comes reward it by praising and fussing. Get the puppy to recognise its name by using it frequently when talking to it. Always use it when calling at meal times. Until it will answer to a name and come when called, further training is virtually impossible. Remember that a young puppy has a very retentive memory, so do everything possible at all times to encourage it to come when called by praising or caressing it, even if prior to coming it has done something it should not have done. If, having called the puppy and got him to come to you, you then scold or punish it, it will inevitably associate the scolding with the action of coming to you and the next time it is called may be very chary of coming in anticipation of another scolding.

A bed of some kind should have been provided before the arrival of the puppy. It may be in a box, basket or bench, of a size and shape to suit the animal it is intended for and the personal preference of the owner. It will serve the dual purpose of bed and resting place and should be situated in a draught-free spot, out of the way of people moving about the room, and be made really comfortable, so that the dog will learn to go to it voluntarily and to stay in it when tired or wanting to rest after play. But, however comfortable this resting place may be made it will take a little time for the puppy to get accustomed to it and to stay in it when told to do so.

The first night in a new home is often a time of trouble. When the lights are put out the youngster may be placed in its bed, stroked and petted and left in the hope that after the excitements of the day it will sleep peacefully through the night. That hope may be fulfilled – perhaps in one case in a hundred! It is much more likely that as soon as left the puppy will start crying or yelping, make frantic efforts to get out of the receptacle in which its bed is placed and, if its protestations are firmly ignored, will howl yet more loudly, eventually becoming hysterical. What is to be done in such circumstances? Perhaps the owner realises after a time that some action must be taken, goes down and by coaxing and fussing tries to persuade the puppy to settle down. As long as it has the comfort of human companionship it will remain quiet and may appear to compose itself for sleep, but as soon as it is again left it will wail and howl as persistently and loudly as ever. Should this happen, on no account succumb to the temptation of scolding the little culprit. It is most unlikely that it will be effective in keeping the puppy quiet. The howls and lamentations will probably be just as loud as before when you go away again, and by your harsh treatment at this time you risk destroying the youngster's confidence and affection which it is so desirable to cultivate. The easy solution is to give in and take the baby up to bed with you. From the puppy's point of view that will probably be quite satisfactory, and both of you may have a quiet night. But unless you are prepared to let him sleep with you permanently, the same problem will have to be faced the next night, and when starting to train any animal it is a golden rule to begin as you mean to go on.

Remember that the puppy which becomes so vociferously miserable when left by itself has hitherto slept snuggled up against its dam or its litter mates, and is missing not only their company but also, and perhaps even more, the warmth of their bodies. A satisfactory way out of the difficulty is to arrange that the box or basket in which the bed is placed has walls sufficiently high to prevent the puppy from clambering out. Or to fit a lid or cover; taking precautions, of course, to ensure that there is ample ventilation. Cover the floor of the box with a cushion or soft mattress of some kind and put in a hot-water bottle for extra comfort. Make the water bottle really hot and cover it completely with a blanket, making sure that there is no risk of the puppy coming into direct contact with the bottle and being burned. A hot-water bottle will give out warmth through the blanket for a long time and the puppy will probably soon snuggle against it and sleep soundly and happily until the morning. Usually the device of providing a warm, cosy sleeping place will work wonders, but when dealing with a particularly young, nervous or distressed puppy, an aspirin or tranquiliser may be given to quieten it and induce sleep. This does not mean that the regular or frequent use of sedatives is recommended. On the contrary, it is much to be deprecated, but in an emergency it is to be preferred to waging a losing battle with an unhappy puppy being put to sleep for the first time alone and in strange surroundings. A box of the type described has the additional advantage of preventing a puppy roaming about during the night should it be wakeful, and making messes on the floor of the room in which it is confined, as a restless youngster is very apt to do.

The use of a playpen-like enclosure in conjunction with the

sleeping box is of the greatest use. It will ensure that the baby is not trodden on when it is unnoticed and enable it to be confined safely when it is left, or after it wakes from a nap during the day. Another advantage is that by being put in its pen fairly frequently a puppy will quickly become accustomed to the idea that its bed is its own special place, be made familiar with its feel and smell and learn to associate it with rest and relaxation as well as with quiet security. It will be more readily trained to go to it when commanded to 'Go to your box' or to 'Lie down'.

A puppy obtained from a kennel may never have been taken into a house and have had no contact with humans other than those who fed it. When brought into a private home it may, therefore, be shy and suspicious of everyone at first, and even when it has come to recognise its owner as a friend and protector may still show fear or uneasiness in the presence of visitors. The more such a puppy is handled and taken into the company of strangers the quicker it will acquire confidence and lose its timidity. As soon as a puppy has been inoculated, at the age of nine or ten weeks, let it be seen and fussed by your friends and visitors and give it a chance of seeing other dogs which are known to be of a friendly disposition. A dog which is shy or nervous with strangers is never a satisfactory pet. As it grows, give it opportunities to widen its mental horizon by taking it to a town on a shopping expedition to get it used to the hustle and bustle of traffic. Let it wear a soft collar but keep it off the ground, and be very careful that it is never roughly handled or frightened. Almost any puppy will grow into a fearless adult if it has learnt in puppyhood to regard humans and other dogs as friends.

Before going on to training proper it may be well to stress the importance of never allowing a puppy to get used to doing something of which you may later disapprove. For example, if you let a puppy beg for scraps at table you cannot reasonably blame it if it still solicits tit-bits at meal times when full grown. Similarly, if a puppy forms the habit of making itself comfortable on sofas or chairs it will later be resentful and indignant if banished from such places because it has grown too big, or has a coat which moults hairs on the upholstery. It may seem quite amusing for a puppy to fawn on its owner and friends, standing on its hind legs and resting its paws on their clothing, but a dog which behaves in this way as an adult and wipes large, muddy feet on visitor's clothes, or terrifies a child by standing against it in affectionate welcome, may cause anger and annoyance. Always be on your guard, therefore, against teaching or allowing your puppy to do anything which is likely to develop into a bad habit.

# CHAPTER THREE

## HOUSE TRAINING

FOR MANY the acquisition of a young puppy is attended by the fear that the business of getting it to be clean in the house must inevitably be difficult, tedious and long drawn out. There is, however, no reason for alarm, for with constant watchfulness, patience and perseverence, training in house manners should not take long and there is certainly nothing difficult about it. Some dogs are much easier than others to train in this respect. A good deal depends on the breed, as well as on the individual, and on the conditions in which the puppy's early infancy has been passed prior to its being taken to its new home.

If it has been reared since birth in a small kennel, kept shut up for long periods and given neither opportunity nor encouragement to urinate or defaecate anywhere except in its living or sleeping quarters, it will naturally have formed the habit of relieving itself there and have no idea of being clean. Normally even very young puppies have a natural instinct to go as far as possible from their bed to empty their bowels or to pass water, and if reared in roomy conditions which are kept properly clean will be very little trouble to teach to go outside, or to whatever place is set aside for their use, rather than mess on the floor or carpet of the room in which they live. For this reason a puppy obtained from a private home is usually easier to train to the house than one from a kennel. Similarly, an older dog which has grown up in a kennel is likely to take much longer to house train than a young puppy, so that the earlier a youngster is taken in hand after it leaves its dam the quicker results will be achieved.

It should be realised from the outset that a puppy has a

comparatively small stomach, needs small meals at fairly frequent intervals and cannot, therefore, be expected to go for lengthy periods without relieving itself. Neither should it be expected to be regular in its motions. From this it follows that it must be carefully watched at all times at first if accidents are to be avoided. If a garden or yard is available the puppy should be put out whenever there is a likelihood of this being necessary. This should be done, for example, first thing in the morning, as soon as it wakes, after every meal, after it has been playing indoors, or resting or sleeping for any considerable time, and last thing at night before being put into its box to sleep. It may be advisable to stress here that it is important to allow a space of at least two hours to elapse between the last meal and bedtime. Many owners make the mistake of giving a puppy that is to sleep in the house a good drink of milk or a dish of sloppy food just before leaving it for the night. The result is that the youngster cannot last out until morning and in consequence misbehaves, leaving a tell-tale puddle or worse as evidence of its lapse.

When you think the puppy ought to go out don't just shut him outside in the hope that he will do what is necessary before he worries to be let in again. The probability is that he will have no idea why he has been banished from the house and left by himself in the open, and will either howl or whine in distress until the door is opened, or wander about aimlessly, then sit shivering awaiting your coming. In either case, the result may well be that the act which he has been put out to perform may occur immediately he is re-admitted indoors. Such a mischance may be prevented by making a point of going into the garden or yard with the puppy and staying with him.

This may mean waiting some minutes, but exercise patience and as soon as the youngster has relieved himself praise him lavishly, making every effort to show him that you are pleased with him, before taking him into the house with you. If this is done consistently your puppy will soon learn to associate being let out with a certain mode of behaviour which is inevitably followed by the reward of being praised and fussed by you. In this way he will quickly conform to a routine which will be more firmly established each time it is repeated. Immediate results are not to be expected. For a few days it will be necessary to be ever on the alert for signs that an accident is about to occur indoors. Immediately the puppy is noticed turning round and round or squatting, admonish him with a sharp NO and take him outdoors at once.

The sound NO is the first command the dog will learn, and it is most important for all future training that the sound should be firmly associated in his mind from ceasing to do, or refraining from doing, something of which you disapprove. The word should never be used needlessly and when it is uttered it must always be in a commanding, but not menacing, tone. Once a puppy has learnt the significance of this sound he has made a big step forwards in preliminary training. Throughout life a dog should automatically obey the injunction implicit in the reproof NO.

Despite the utmost vigilance, accidents are almost sure to happen occasionally during the first week or so. In such an event do not smack the puppy or threaten it in any way. If you do he will associate being punished with performing a perfectly natural and necessary function, and may be cowed or bemused by being chastised for no apparent reason. The next time he wants to relieve himself he will probably hide in a corner or under the furniture. If you are able to catch him in the act say NO sharply, scold him and put him outside. While he is away the mess should be cleared up and the surrounding area thoroughly rubbed with a disinfectant or sprinkled with pepper. The reason for this is that it is natural for a dog to return to a spot smelling of urine or faeces when it wants to relieve himself again, and to leave a smelly spot on the carpet or floor is to tempt him to repeat the transgression in the same place. If a puppy is kept in a flat or building without access to a garden, a tray or heap of sawdust, wood shavings, dry earth or torn-up paper may be made to serve the purpose. The routine to be followed is much the same. Place the puppy on the tray at frequent intervals instead of taking him outside, watching him and preventing him from wandering until he has done what is required. Keep the tray in the same place at all times so that the puppy may get to know where to go.

A difficulty often experienced is that even if accidents are prevented by ceaseless vigilance during the day, the puppy cannot be controlled during the night. Even when fairly reliable by day it may be unable to last from bedtime to the next morning. The best way to overcome this is to put the puppy to sleep in a deep-sided box, or in a receptacle with a lid or cover, as recommended in the last chapter. This will keep him confined to the bed and obviate the danger of his wandering and making messes when left alone. A tray of sawdust or earth, as previously described, is also a great help in a home where a garden is available in the day time. Not only will it serve to teach the puppy to be clean by night as well as by day, it will also be of great use during spells of bad weather or in times of sickness. Many small pet dogs object strongly to going out before being put to bed when it is raining heavily or a cold, boisterous wind is blowing, even when they are considered house trained. For these an indoor sanitary tray is a valuable supplement to the garden or yard that is generally used.

A puppy which has been trained to be clean in one room may not be equally safe in other rooms, especially in rooms which are unfamiliar to him. It is bound to take some time for him to understand that he is required to be clean in all parts of the house or, indeed, anywhere indoors. Do not fail, therefore, to be specially alert with a puppy allowed access to parts of the house other than the room in which he has had his first schooling. The early stages of house training may be very trying and time consuming, but it is well worth the sacrifice of time and leisure to get a puppy over the first obstacles quickly without destroying his confidence or frightening him. With patience he will soon learn to go to the door and ask for it to be opened, or make a bee-line for his tray of his own accord. Be ever watchful, for it is vitally important that the association being formed in the youngster's mind should not be broken. If his pleas go unnoticed and the door remains shut, he may be forced to transgress, and this may have the effect of undoing much of what has already been accomplished in house training.

It is impossible to estimate how long it will take to teach a young dog to be clean in the house. So much depends on the animal concerned and on the training ability of the owner. Usually a three months' old puppy may be taught house manners in a fortnight. Some respond much more quickly. The key to success is to carry out training systematically, exercising patience, vigilance and common sense at all times.

The advantages of providing a playpen has already been mentioned. Such an enclosure is also a great asset when training is being given in house cleanliness. If, when a puppy has to be left by itself for a time, either during the day or at night, sheets of paper are spread on the floor of the pen, the puppy will use them rather than soil his bed. This will serve the double purpose of preventing messes on carpet or floor and get him accustomed to relieving himself on paper when access to the outside or a tray is denied him. Many puppies will have learnt to use paper in this way before coming to a new home. It is common practice for breeders to put newspaper on the floor of an indoor kennel beyond the position of the bed or nest itself and, as soon as they are strong enough to stand, quite small whelps will creep out of their sleeping compartment to urinate or defaecate on the paper.

If after having learnt to be clean indoors an older puppy should misbehave, firm correction must be given. But before scolding him harshly be quite sure that the culprit understands why he is being punished and that the offence for which you are correcting him was deliberate and not the result of your own carelessness in not noticing the puppy's request to be let out.

All puppies like to bite and tear any article which appeals to them and often chew upholstered furniture, mats, carpets or shoes unless firmly checked. The desire to bite or nibble anything which comes their way arises partly from playfulness and partly from the need to exercise the jaws and help the teeth to grow. The best way to prevent household possessions from being damaged is to provide toys of some kind which a puppy can bite, chew and worry to his heart's content and learn to regard as his own property. Anything of suitable size that is chewable will be accepted readily and come to be greatly prized. A piece of stout rag or sacking knotted into a compact shape, a stuffed leather glove or old slipper are all suitable. But perhaps the most convenient and safest toys to supply are a raw knuckle bone of a size suitable for the puppy to which it is given, a solid rubber ball, rubber bone or rubber ring. Precautions must be taken to see that the ball, bone or ring is made of hard, solid rubber and not likely to be affected by being chewed by the puppy's sharp teeth. Some toys of this kind sold for dogs, though they appear to be solid, consist of a layer of hard rubber covering an inner core of rubber sponge. The solid skin is liable to be torn and fragments of the softer interior pulled off. If these pieces are swallowed they may seriously injure the puppy. It is necessary, therefore, to make sure that the article is really hard and solid before letting a puppy have it to gnaw. A raw knuckle bone is the best of all toys. After it has been played with, take it up, rinse well in cold water, then put it in an oven until it is thoroughly hard and crisp again. Treated in this way one bone will last a long time and each time it is given to the puppy will be received as rapturously as though it were new.

Encourage the puppy to play with its toys, to take them to its box and even to sleep with them. The more he plays with them the more he will value them, and they will do much to comfort him when he is left alone. If he starts chewing or biting a carpet or furnishings, correct him immediately. Gently disengage his teeth, say NO firmly and sharply and give him one of his toys. Do this consistently. Never let a lapse go uncorrected – provided, of course, you catch the puppy in the act of misbehaving. It is worse than useless to correct him for something he did before you caught him. If you do this he will not understand the reason for the scolding and his bewilderment may tend to undermine his trust in you. When you actually catch him while he is biting or tearing something he should not, say no sharply at once and if he desists praise him enthusiastically. Do not at first place temptation in his way unnecessarily. When a puppy is left alone he is pretty sure to chew furnishings and other things in the room in which he is confined if given the chance. Before leaving him, therefore, put him in his playpen or similar enclosure with his toys. He will then be out of mischief and will probably settle down quietly.

CHAPTER FOUR

# *LEAD TRAINING AND OUTDOOR COMPANIONSHIP*

A PUPPY should not be taken for walks until at least four months old. With many breeds it is better to wait another two months. Before this age the body is not strong enough and the bones too soft to stand the strain of road exercise. It is a common but depressing sight to meet a two- or three-months' old puppy being dragged along a street at the end of a lead by a well-intentioned owner who fails to realise that to take so young a puppy walking on a hard road is almost sure to have an adverse effect on its development, and may spoil its conformation for life. Let a young puppy have plenty of opportunity to romp and play in the open air when the weather is suitable, but never let it get over tired. This does not mean that training to collar and lead should be left until road walking is to begin. On the contrary, the earlier a dog becomes used to wearing a collar and going happily on a lead the better. As a general rule, it may be said that the longer he is left before being made familiar with the feeling of being restrained by a lead and to walk willingly under its control, the more difficult he will be to train.

The first step is to accustom the puppy to wearing a collar. This may be done by fastening a soft, light collar about the neck, being careful that it is not too tight for comfort nor loose enough to be scratched off. You may start at any age from eight weeks onwards. At first the puppy may object, being irked or worried by the sensation of having his neck encircled. To minimise this it is advisable to put the collar on just before romping or playing with the youngster, so that his attention may be distracted. Leave the collar on for an hour or two and stop any attempts to scratch or rub it off by a sharp, admonitory no. Put the collar on at intervals for a few days, after which it will probably be worn without signs of discomfort or resentment. When that stage is reached a light lead or cord may be attached and left lying on the ground, so that it is dragged about by the puppy. Be very careful that the lead is not heavy enough to interfere with the puppy's movements and only leave it attached to the collar at times when you or someone else is present to see that it does not get entangled in an obstacle of any kind. The aim is to impart the idea that the use of a collar and lead does not entail discomfort. It is, therefore, important to ensure that the puppy is never frightened or perturbed by being suddenly jerked or pulled up by the lead being caught on a bush, piece of furniture or the like.

When the puppy accepts the collar and lead as a matter of course, which it should do in a matter of a few days, quietly pick up the end of the lead and let him pull against it as he plays. Then try to persuade him to follow you as you move away from him, calling him by name. If he refuses to follow or pulls away or bites the lead, talk to him in an encouraging voice and try to attract him by showing him a tit-bit. If he responds to the gentle control of the lead praise him, but if he persists in pulling stubbornly away or is obstinate, admonishment him with a sharp no. Be very patient but determined, and continue to practise this simple form of training until you succeed in getting the pupil to walk in the direction taken by you without being pulled. Most puppies learn very quickly but should you encounter difficulties do not persist with the lesson too long. It is much better to suspend a session after a comparatively short time if a puppy seems to be obdurate, panicky or tired, than to go on at the risk of his learning to associate being put on the lead with unpleasant compulsion.

When some progress has been made, it will help if you can get a friend to assist you. Hold the puppy on a fairly loose lead while your assistant calls him from a short distance away, at the same time trying to attract him by holding out a tempting tit-bit. The puppy will probably run forwards. As he does so follow him, still holding the lead but keeping it slightly taut, so that he feels a slight but steady pull on the collar. Repeat this as often as is necessary; gradually increasing the distance from which he is called. Then try to make him follow you as you walk in the opposite direction, urging him forwards if necessary by calling him and by gentle promptings from the lead. In this way he will soon get used to lead control and respond without opposition to your movements. If begun at an early age progress in most cases will be rapid, but do not try to hurry this preliminary training unduly. Sometimes, as when dealing with a naturally rebellious or timid puppy, success may seem slow in being achieved, but with patient perseverance and understanding almost any youngster may be taught to go well on a lead in ten days or a fortnight.

As has been said, a puppy should not be taken for road walks until he is at least four months old, but there are many advantages in lead training him at a much younger age. Perhaps the most important of these is that he will be very much easier to control when eventually he is taken out for definite walks than if training has to be started from the beginning at that time. It may also be very useful, especially in the case of young puppies of the larger breeds which are too big or heavy to be conveniently carried, if you wish to take your dog visiting on a short expedition which entails only a little walking. A lead trained puppy of any age is much more easily managed away from its home than one which has no idea of lead control.

When the time comes for a puppy to be taken for a walk on a road the excitement of his novel surroundings may make him riotous, so that he forgets his earlier training and pulls violently forwards, straining and panting in such a way that the walk becomes a sort of struggle between him and his handler. This behaviour must be strongly discouraged. We are all too familiar with the sight of the dog which gives the impression that he is taking his owner for a walk! This is a sure indication that proper lead training has not been given. The best way to deal with a dog which persists in pulling instead of going comfortably on a slightly slack lead, is to shorten the lead, draw him close and give the command BACK. If this is not successful use a folded newspaper and hold it in front of the dog, tapping him lightly on the nose each time he lunges or tries to pull forwards, accompanying each tap with the command BACK. This method usually succeeds, but a very lusty or determined youngster may be undeterred and either treat the setting up of a barrier and nose tapping as a game, or seize the folded paper and bite or tear it. Should this happen stronger measures must be adopted. Keep the dog on a short lead and each time he pulls forwards jerk the lead strongly to bring him back, admonishing him at the same time by uttering the command sharply and loudly. Follow this procedure consistently until the dog learns that pulling forwards against the lead is always productive of discomfort. Do not fail to praise him well immediately improvement is shown.

A nervous or timid puppy which has gone very satisfactorily on the lead in a garden may be so upset when he finds himself on the road for the first time that he insists on sitting down and refusing to move. The remedy is to stop, stroke him, speak to him in a friendly tone and try to persuade him to follow you. Do not drag him along in a sitting position. That treatment will only add to his nervousness. If necessary, pick him up and carry him for a short distance, soothing and reassuring him by talking to him quietly. When he seems to have regained confidence, put him down and try again. This kind of thing is not likely to happen if a puppy is taken about in his owner's arms while he is still too young to walk. He will then get used to the noise of traffic, strange scents and hurrying pedestrians, without fear or apprehension, gaining a sense of security by being held by friendly protective arms. When later he is taken for a road walk on a lead he will be unaffected by unfamiliar noises and the presence of strangers.

The urgent importance of training a puppy to answer to its name and to come immediately it is called, has been stressed in a previous chapter. If this willing and spontaneous response to being called is instilled in a young puppy there will be little risk that when first released from the lead in an open space he will prove unmanageable and refuse to return when called. Failure to respond to a call when running free is rarely a sign of wilful disobedience. It usually signifies lack of proper train-ing, or want of sympathy between dog and owner. If your dog ignores your summons when called from a distance, on no account lose your head and start running after him. That will only add to your difficulties, since the puppy will think this is some sort of new game and run as fast as he can in the opposite direction. Instead, call him in a loud voice and, having attracted his attention, turn and begin running away from him, or keep facing him and move quickly backwards. Con-tinue to go away from him but go on calling him and make encouraging gestures. It is safe to assume that your dog is just as anxious not to lose you as you are not to lose him and, seeing you getting further and further away will soon come running back. Immediately he comes to you praise and reward him. This must be done however angry you may be. Remember that your dog cannot reason from cause to effect and if you punish him on his return he will associate that punishment, not with being disobedient in refusing to come when called, but with coming up to you. The result may be that the next time he is called he will be very unwilling to respond because of the association formed in his mind between returning to you and being punished.

If after such an experience you feel it is unsafe to let your dog off the lead in case you cannot get him to come back, the best thing is to take him to a park or other open space and put him on a very long lead – the usual lead may be lengthened by tying a piece of cord to it. Let the dog go to the full length

Getting used to collar and lead (Jack Russel Pup)

Press with hand on back to sit

of the lead and after a time call him. If he turns attract him to you by offering him a tit-bit or by making coaxing sounds. Praise and fuss him immediately he responds. If he shows no inclination to come to your call, pull him towards you steadily by shortening the lead, calling him all the time and doing everything you can to encourage him to come to you. When he does, reward him by fussing and showing him that you are pleased with him. Continue this training until he will come to you at once and without fail when you call him. Practise this frequently, both when the dog is at home in the garden or on a road walk, as well as in a park or field. Time devoted to perfecting an instant response to your call under all conditions is well spent, for once this is thoroughly learnt all further training will be greatly simplified.

Nearly all dogs enjoy motoring and most owners like to take their pet with them when making a journey by car. Until he is used to travelling a puppy or young dog may be sick after being in a vehicle for a short time. This trouble is usually quickly got over, but in some cases it may persist unless special measures are taken to cure it. As a precaution, do not give any food for at least an hour before starting a journey. Half an hour or so before setting out dose the dog with glucose, using a heaped teaspoonful of the powder dissolved in two spoonfuls of water. If the puppy seems very prone to car sickness repeat the dose after about half an hour's travelling. Some of the anti-sickness tablets specially manufactured for travel-sick dogs are convenient, reliable and safe. If a dog is to be a pleasant and trouble-free companion in a car some training is usually necessary. Some individuals give very little trouble from the first, but a rampageous or excitable youngster may be a nuisance or a danger through jumping about, barking at passing traffic or in other ways distracting the driver's attention. A dog which behaves in that way should be relegated to the back seat and secured by two leads, each rather shorter than the car's width, one being attached to either side of the car. Barking must be checked and the habit of pushing the head out of the window firmly corrected. Wind or dust may cause injury to the dog's eyes and seriously impair the sight. A puppy should never be allowed to travel on the floor of a car. This is likely to cause sickness or fainting from petrol fumes or over-heated air.

# CHAPTER FIVE

# TRAINING TO SIT AND LIE DOWN
# ON COMMAND

AFTER a puppy has learnt house manners and become used to going well on the lead, perhaps the most useful lesson it can be taught is to sit or lie down when told to do so. Either may be taught easily and quickly. The Sit is taught by placing the puppy standing, with the right hand on its throat to support the head. Now press the quarters downwards with the left hand, forcing the youngster into a sitting posture, at the same time saying SIT. If the puppy tries to get up press it down again and repeat the command SIT. When he remains sitting quietly under compulsion for a few moments praise him or give him a tit-bit as a reward, but be sure he received this reward while sitting. If you let him get up before giving him the tit-bit he may associate the reward with the act of rising and not with staying in the sitting position.

The lesson should be repeated several times, with a short break and a reward after each successful effort. Continue the procedure consistently each day, never making a training session too long but persevering until the puppy assumes the required posture without having to be pressed into position on the command SIT. With kindness, firmness and patience an ordinarily biddable puppy should learn to sit on command in three or four days.

When he has reached that stage and is obeying promptly and reliably, the giving of tit-bits may be dispensed with. To show him clearly that you are pleased with him each time he responds to your command will be sufficient reward. When he has learnt to sit when told to in one place, continue the exercise elsewhere, both in the house and in the open, until he will sit anywhere immediately he hears the command SIT.

A puppy which has been thoroughly trained in this way will be much easier to control at all times than one which has not, and will respond more readily to other, later forms of training. Furthermore, a young puppy is much more easily handled when being taught to Sit than is a fully grown dog, especially in the larger breeds.

To train a puppy to lie down on command a similar procedure may be followed. First press the dog into the prone position by placing the hands on the withers and the rump and gently forcing him down. As he goes down utter the word DOWN firmly and clearly. If he tries to get up press him down again, repeating the command DOWN. When he is lying quietly lift the hands slightly so that he no longer feels that he is under pressure. Immediately he tries to rise press him down again, ordering DOWN as pressure is reapplied. When he relaxes and shows an inclination to remain in position gently praise and reward him. Be careful, however, not to praise him in a way likely to excite him or to make him think the lesson is over. As mentioned when dealing with training to Sit, it is essential to make the dog associate being rewarded with the act of lying down and not with getting up. Another method of getting a dog to lie down, and one which is easier with some animals than the one already described, is to make him sit then draw his forelegs forwards, thus bringing the body on to the ground, uttering the command DOWN as you draw the forelegs towards you.

Preliminary training should be given in a quiet, secluded spot, away from distractions and though, as in all forms of training, firmness and determination are necessary, every effort must be made to prevent the dog being frightened or made resentful or panicky. If you use unnecessary force or are unduly rough in getting the dog down, he will probably struggle to get up and what should be an exercise in discipline may degenerate into an undignified tussle which may have the effect of turning the dog against all further training. Keep the first lessons short. As soon as the slightest progress has been made – that is when the dog relaxes and stops trying to get up for a few seconds – praise him and let him get up for a break. Repeat the practice a number of times during the session and be meticulous in carrying out the training every day, or oftener, until you have the pupil lying down on command wherever he may be. When dealing with a particularly unruly puppy, or an older dog, it is sometimes convenient at first to keep him on the lead when teaching him to lie down on command, but most puppies may be taught without being placed under such restraint. Don't be discouraged when teaching the Sit or Down if, after he has become responsive when pressed into position, your puppy makes no attempt to obey your command when you try to get him to act without touching him.

You should realise that for him there are two quite separate phases to this training, and he can only learn one at a time. Your first task is to teach him to associate the sound Sit or Down with taking up a certain pose under pressure from your hands. The second is to make him understand that he must go into position on your word of command without being touched at all. If training is given correctly, a dog that has become thoroughly proficient in the first exercise will learn the second without much difficulty, but allowances must be made for him to adjust his mental association from the first to the second phase of this training.

When making your first efforts to teach your dog to lie down without being touched, stand close to him, as you did when teaching him to sit or lie down under compulsion. Don't try to get him to obey your command from a distance until he has reached the stage when he will lie down when told without fail when you are standing by him. Having got so far, practise the exercise at odd times whenever your dog is with you, but never forget to reward him when he does as he is told by showing him that his compliance pleases you. As training proceeds keep him in the down position for longer periods before letting him get up.

A dog which lives in the house in close association with his owner or family will be a much more pleasant companion after he has learnt to sit or lie down on command. If, for example, he seems to becoming over excited or starts jumping up against children or visitors, he may be quietened at once by being given the command SIT. Any dog which has been allowed to form the habit of jumping up boisterously to greet its owner or friends may be made to behave more decorously immediately it has been trained to respond to the word SIT or DOWN.

When he has been taught to be clean in the house, to come when called by name, to refrain from biting and tearing household articles, to walk properly on a lead and to sit or lie down if told to do so, a young puppy may be considered to have absorbed as much education as can reasonably be expected. The more advanced types of training which are dealt with in future chapters should be left until the dog is from nine to twelve months old. Any puppy which has been thoroughly taught the elements of socialisation as outlined in the first five chapters of this handbook will prove an adept pupil when the time comes to continue his training.

CHAPTER SIX

# *WALKING TO HEEL AND HALTING*
# *ON COMMAND*

WHEN TRAINING a puppy to walk on a lead without pulling, the command BACK may be used to curb any tendency to lunge forwards and strain against the leash. Later it may be desired to teach him to walk at heel, that is keep close behind his owner, and to remain there until released by the word FREE. Start with the dog walking freely in his usual manner, held on a fairly short lead. While walking try to attract his attention by calling him by name and encourage him to come nearer by patting your thigh and saying HEEL sharply and clearly. When he comes pat him and praise him and try to get him to remain at your side. Immediately he tries to run forward give the command HEEL again and repeat the motions to attract him. If necessary, keep him in the correct position by shortening the lead. Reward him generously as soon as he shows any signs of keeping his place as you continue to walk, but admonish every attempt to get in front of you by a stern repetition of the word HEEL, at the same time pointing to your foot to indicate where he should be.

If this mode of treatment is ineffectual and the dog persists in pulling forward each time he is got into position, he must be made to understand that it is more comfortable for him to obey your command than to try to get his own way. As he lunges forward pull him up sharply by a jerk of the lead, simultaneously uttering HEEL and patting your thigh. Give him a pat or praise him when he is in the right position, but do not excite him while praising him and keep him at heel while you talk to him. Then walk on. Repeat this exercise frequently and regularly until your dog will come to heel without any inducement other than the word of command.

It is very important to guard against making walking to heel distasteful to the dog. Be sure to retain his confidence and gaiety the whole time he is under instruction. Otherwise your pupil may consider walking at heel as some kind of punishment, and always look miserable or dejected when commanded to keep in that position. If, however, you stroke and talk encouragingly to him at intervals as he walks, he will realise that there is nothing to make him apprehensive in being required to walk close to you. In this way obeying the command HEEL will not be associated in his mind with discomfort or irksome restraint. The aim is to have your dog walking close behind you quietly but looking gay and alert; not slouching along with a hangdog expression, as though he is fearful of being thrashed if he leaves you. Do not keep him at heel for too long at a time. Let each lesson be short, but do not let up until your dog makes some show of understanding what you want and gives some indication of doing what is required of him.

The strength of the inducement necessary to make a dog walk at heel on command will vary according to the temperament of the individual being trained. With a dog which is by nature gentle and anxious to please, a slight pull on the lead accompanied by the command HEEL may be all that is needed or desirable to remind him of the position he is to take up. But with a rougher, more rebellious type a sharp jerk of the lead with a sternly uttered command must be applied and it may be necessary to repeat this compulsion every time he attempts to get in front. Early lessons in walking to heel should be given in a quiet place, where there is little traffic and few distractions to attract the dogs attention. Always walk at a brisk pace. This will make walking at heel more easy and comfortable for your dog than a slower movement. Once he shows that he understands clearly what the command HEEL means, practise it often whenever you are out with him.

*Slip-lead for puppy training*

Colour photos by Anne Cumbers

*Boxers are good with kids*

*Training to fetch*

*Obedience training*

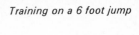

*Training on a 6 foot jump*

*Obedience*

*Sheepdogs at work on a fell farm*

*Police dogs at demonstration*

But don't overdo it and make every possible effort to get the dog to regard the exercise as an enjoyable diversion during an ordinary walk. You must, however, insist on immediate obedience every time you use the word of command and end a lesson only when your dog has done something to justify you in rewarding him with praise. Always remember that to your dog a walk with you is, or should be, a joyous experience. It probably represents a highlight in his daily routine. On no account let training him to walk to heel become so irksome as to spoil his pleasure in accompanying you on an outing. At the termination of a session let him romp and play without restraint, to avoid any risk of a feeling of resentment being formed in connection with the command HEEL.

At first it may be necessary to keep the lead short and fairly tight when bringing a dog to heel, but as progress is made reduce the tautness, only applying pressure when he attempts to leave his position, saying HEEL sharply at the same time. Your aim is to accustom him to walk at heel on a loose lead and training should be given with this in mind. A timid or very sensitive dog may at first tend to hang back after being brought to heel. If this occurs, do not make the mistake of dragging him up to you. Instead, stop and try to attract him by words of encouragement, fussing and praising him when he comes to you. Try to keep him near you by caressing him and speaking to him in a soothing tone, thereby imparting a feeling of confidence and banishing any fear or apprehension he may associate with the restraint you are placing on him. With a dog of this kind progress may at first appear to be very slow, but it is most important that he should not be hurried or cowed, otherwise, even when he has learnt to walk to heel as required, he may always do so unwillingly and look miserable when in that position.

As has already been explained, early lessons in walking to heel on a lead should be given in quiet surroundings, where neither frequent traffic nor passing pedestrians or dogs are likely to interfere with the pupil's concentration. Later, however, he should be practised in busier places. Should the dog be tempted by something to leave the heel position, he must be pulled back by a jerk of the lead, given the command HEEL and spoken to sharply with the object of attracting his attention away from the distraction and reconcentrating it on you. Immediately he responds fondle him and encourage him, verbally and by patting your thigh, to follow you closely as before. This training should be continued daily until the dog can be relied on to walk in the desired position wherever he may be and to ignore diversions of all kinds. It will be some time before this training is perfected, but be patient and persistent until it is. Until your dog is thoroughly reliable in walking to heel while on the lead it is folly to attempt to train him to react to your command while he is running loose.

When the time comes to teach the next phase of the exercise, it is best to begin with the dog walking to heel on the lead in the way to which he is accustomed. Quietly remove the lead and continue to walk forward as before, speaking encouragingly to hold the dog's attention and keep him from going off. Should he run forward or hold back attract him by patting the thigh and saying HEEL. If he returns to position praise him well, but if he goes off call him by name and giving the command HERE. Fuss him immediately he comes to you, then point to your foot and command HEEL. If he has been well trained to walk steadily to heel on the lead there should be very little difficulty in getting him to remain at heel when the lead is removed, but if he behaves badly when free put him back on the lead and give him further practice on walking to heel on a really slack lead. When he seems to be really proficient in this try him again without the lead.

When he is under good command let him run freely for a time, then attract his attention by calling him by name, pat your thigh and command HEEL. Reward him well when he comes, then keep him at heel for a few minutes. Whenever he fails to obey your command while running loose put him on the lead and get him walking to heel as before. Do not fail to praise him when he comes to your call, even though he may not go to heel at once. Walking to heel off the lead will be learnt in time by any dog, providing he is first trained to be completely reliable on the lead and that nothing is ever done to interfere with his association of pleasure with coming to you in any circumstances. When your dog is walking to heel off the lead you may use the word FREE to indicate that he is now released from the command to walk close by your side or behind you. Always utter this word in a cheerful voice, and it is a good idea to accompany it with a wave of the hand – a signal which your dog will soon learn to recognise and appreciate.

Having taught your dog heel work it may be useful to make him understand the significance of the command HALT. This is very easily done. While walking him at heel on the lead give the command HALT and stand still, at the same time checking the dog's movement with the lead. Repeat this several times, rewarding or praising the dog when he shows signs of stopping at the sound HALT without further prompting. It will help considerably if you make the halt with military precision, stamping the foot on the ground as the command HALT is given. Let the cessation of movement be sharp and decisive, so that your dog is able to understand at once what your command signifies. If you wish, you can later combine the Halt with the Sit, with which your dog will already be familiar. If the command SIT is always given immediately following HALT, in time the dog will form the habit of sitting as soon as he halts and thereafter the word SIT may be dropped. When the dog has been trained to halt and sit while on the lead he may be quickly taught to respond to the same command when loose.

A final word of advice on training in heel work. Regularity and consistency are essential if success is to be achieved. It is very unreasonable to expect a young dog to learn to walk close to its owner, keeping to the same relative position until released, if he is sometimes exercised without any sort of control and at others suddenly brought under rigid discipline. Until he is really proficient at walking to heel on the lead he should have daily practice, and instruction should always be given by the same person. Later he will probably respond satisfactorily to commands given by anyone he knows well, but during the formative period he should have but one tutor.

# CHAPTER SEVEN

# *STAYING IN ONE POSITION*

IN A PREVIOUS chapter instructions on how to teach a puppy to sit or lie down on command were given. Practice in this exercise should be continued as he grows up, so that he gets used to obeying the words of command at all times and in all places. So far he has been taught to sit or lie down when the owner is standing near, and required to remain in position for very short periods. The next step is to lengthen the time during which he will sit or lie still, making him understand that he must stay down until he is told to get up.

Whether you train him to sit or lie down is a matter for your own personal choice. In general, however, for ordinary purposes it is better to let him lie down when you intend to keep him stationary for longer than a few minutes, as a dog is much more comfortable in that position than if made to sit for any considerable time. First get him in the required posture by giving the usual word of command. Stay by him but immediately he begins to get up before told to do so press him down and repeat the command DOWN. Keep on with this until the dog remains down until you tell him he may get up. Do not be impatient, and remember that it is far better to get the dog to stay down for a minute or so before being told to get up than to have him constantly rising of his own accord through boredom after a much longer period.

As soon as he remains down quietly praise him, but be sure to do this while he is still down. If you reward him in any way after he has got up, there is a strong likelihood that he will associate the reward with the act of getting up and your efforts to teach him to stay down on command will be wasted. A dog which has learnt to obey the command SIT or LIE

DOWN as a puppy will quickly learn to stay in position for longer periods without giving much trouble. Should any difficulty be encountered, the lesson may be given on the lead. Get the pupil down beside you and place a foot on the lead in such a way that he cannot rise without feeling the pull of the lead on his collar. Proceed as before, meeting every effort to rise with an admonishing NO. This correction, supplemented by a jerk from the lead, will soon build up an association of discomfort with the effort to rise, and the dog will quickly realise that it is more comfortable to stay still by you than to get up while under your command to stay down.

At first it is best to have the dog lying close by your side as you stand ready to forestall any move he makes to get up. But when some progress has been made, practice may be given in the home while you are sitting down doing something near, and in full view of, the dog or having a meal. Gradually extend the time the dog is required to stay down and when he has reached the stage of being obedient while you sit or stand near him, get him used to your moving about and away from him. Remain fairly close, however, so that he will not be tempted to move by the fear that you will leave him.

When you think he is ready, practise the exercise out of doors, at first moving from one side of him to the other, or going a little way in front of him. Check any inclination to get up by holding up a warning finger and using an admonitory NO. When he stays still for a short time go to him quietly and reward him. Do not call him to you before rewarding him. If you do he will associate being rewarded with running up to you – which is what he wants to do anyway! If he gets up and comes towards you, go to him at once, reprove him with a sharp NO and take him back to the spot where you left him and command DOWN. When he is again lying quietly try again. Continue this exercise regularly, gradually lengthening the period during which the dog is kept down.

When he can be relied on to stay down until told he may

rise, practise moving about while he is lying down. Pass backwards and forwards in front of him, walk round and step across him, always watching him closely and being ready to reprove him with a sharp NO or STAY if he rises or attempts to follow you. Later put him through this lesson in a place where there are passers-by and other sights to divert his attention. Concentrate on making him thoroughly trustworthy in remaining down even in the presence of moving strangers and unfamiliar sounds; steadily obeying your command until you release him from this compulsion.

Next increase the distance you move away from him after having commanded him to lie down. At first it is advisable to back away facing the dog, keeping him steady with an upraised finger and a stern NO if he shows any sign of leaving his position. Remember, if he does move towards you, to go to him at once and take him back to his original place and again command DOWN. If he stays until you have gone some distance away, call the dog to you with the word HERE, making motions of encouragement and attraction. As soon as he reaches you praise him generously. Always bear in mind that, though in teaching this exercise it is essential to arrest any inclination to leave the down position before told to do so, it is vital to refrain from doing anything to make him associate the act of coming to you with discomfort or fear of being punished. Be sure, therefore, that when you call him his coming is made joyous by praise, fussing or reward. Nothing indicates faulty training and lack of understanding between trainer and pupil more clearly than the sight of a dog which, when recalled after an exercise, comes towards his owner with head and tail down and an air of uncertainty as to the reception he is going to get.

Having got your dog really reliable at 'staying put' while you go some distance away from him, the next, and much more difficult, step is to teach him to stay lying quietly at command even when you go out of sight. Start training for this exercise in a place where there are trees, tall bushes, a building or similar cover. Get the dog in the down position and move away as usual, but when at a suitable distance go behind a tree or round the side of a building. Remain out of sight only for a second or two, then reappear. Despite his previous training the dog's natural impulse on losing sight of you will be to get up and come to find you. If he has risen or moved when you come from hiding, go to him, put him back in position repeating DOWN or STAY. Now try again, keeping watch on your dog even while you are hidden from him and return at once to correct him if he moves. Repeat this as often as may be necessary, being very careful at first not to worry the dog by being out of his sight for long at a time. When he remains lying quietly while you are away, go to him and praise him lavishly.

At this stage it is advisable to return to the dog to praise him when he has done well, rather than to call him to you before fussing him, so that he understands clearly that the reward is for staying and not for running up to you. Increase the time you remain hidden very gradually, so that, after his initial uncertainty, your dog soon realises that your absence is only temporary and that there is no fear that you will desert him. In subsequent lessons make a point of using different hiding places and, as your dog becomes accustomed to the exercise, try to correct him if he moves from a distance; saying NO or DOWN loudly and accompanying your command with a downward sweep of your hand.

To perfect a dog in staying down on command until released is merely a matter of frequent repetition, increasing the distance you move away and the time during which you are out of sight. When he is reliable and steady in this you may teach him to come to you on the call of HERE or COME as you reappear from a distant hide. You must be very careful to see that he never leaves his position to come to you before you call him. He must learn to stay down, whether you are in sight or not, until released from his position by your word of command.

Sit and Stay

Trained to be helpfull (Bearded Collie)

Next you may train him to assume the down posture when told to do so while he is moving. The easiest way to do this is give the usual command DOWN, move away some distance then call the dog up to you and as he approaches again give the command DOWN. If he obeys, go to him and praise him. If he does not act on the command, go to him and put him in the down position. Then leave him, call him and as he comes repeat the order DOWN. It may be necessary to repeat this quite often before he responds while moving, but do not overdo this practice, otherwise you may spoil his obedience to the ordinary down and stay and make him apprehensive of coming to you when called. It is advisable not to try to make him go down each time he comes to you after being released from a stay, so that the feeling of pleasure which he has learnt to associate with your call is not interfered with. At first, practise this only now and then and be sure to praise the dog exuberantly when he does as commanded, but do not punish him if he fails to do so. Instead go to him quietly, get him to lie down, move off from a good distance, call him and as he comes again order him down in a loud voice. This exercise may call for much patience and perseverance to make the dog completely reliable, but once he has learnt it thoroughly and will go down at any time, in any place and under any conditions, he will be very easy to control in any emergency.

When trying to make a dog lie down on a word of command given from a distance, always accompany it with a downward sweep of the arm. If you do this your dog will in time respond to the visual signal only and thenceforth be under more certain control if you are so far away as to be almost out of hearing. Once the down and stay has been taught you may introduce all sorts of variants to make an outing more interesting and more enjoyable. For example, having commanded your dog to lie down you may go away, hide, then call his name, to attract his attention, followed by the word HERE or COME, leaving him to enjoy the excitement of finding you.

Play of this kind is an excellent introduction to more serious training in tracking (*see* page 56) should you wish to train your dog for that purpose. In this connection it may be well to emphasise that a dog should be called by name only when it is necessary to attract his attention. To call him to you always use a special word, like HERE or COME. Though actually an inducement, this will soon come to have the significance of a command and be acted on at once.

# CHAPTER EIGHT

# *FETCHING AND CARRYING*

TRAINING in fetching a thrown object and bringing it back may be started at any time after a puppy has learnt the elementary lessons of answering to its name, and is showing recognition of and attachment to his owner. Almost all healthy puppies have an instinctive desire to chase a small object which moves away from them, and this natural inclination may be taken advantage of in instruction in fetching and carrying. The object thrown may be an old glove, a knotted rag, a stuffed skin or anything else of a size, shape and texture which the puppy can pick up and carry without difficulty, or that will not be uncomfortable for it to hold in the mouth. Start off by playing with the youngster, thereby interesting him in the dummy. Let him get used to taking it in his mouth while it is still being held by you. Now throw it a short distance. The dog will probably run after it and pick it up. If he shows no inclination to do so after several tries, tie the object to a length of string and drag it after you, at the same time calling and encouraging the puppy to follow. Then pick it up and play with the puppy again. Repeat this until he joins in the game with zest and chases and picks up the object of his own accord. As soon as he has become sufficiently interested to run after the dummy when it is thrown and picks it up he will have mastered the first step in retrieving.

When he has picked up the object the puppy's first act will probably be either to run off with it or to carry it to his bed or box, there to bite and tear it. This must be countered by calling the pupil by name and making encouraging gestures to attract him to you. On no account chase him in an attempt to make him surrender the object. Such action on your part will be interpreted by the puppy as being part of a more exciting aspect of the game – and one which he is pretty sure to win! Instead, keep on calling him in a persuasive manner and do everything you can think of to tempt him to come to you. Immediately he does so praise him lavishly, gently take the object and give him an attractive tit-bit in exchange. If he is disinclined to give up the object do not try to pull it from his mouth or tussle for its possession. Gently open the jaws and ease it from the teeth, speaking encouragingly and soothingly the while. Now throw the object again and repeat the performance. Be sure to praise and reward the puppy each time he comes to you with the object, but never offer any kind of tit-bit unless he comes to you. A normally intelligent puppy will very soon learn to associate bringing the dummy to you with being rewarded and will return regularly and quickly each time the object is thrown. Should the puppy carry the object to his box instead of bringing it back, place yourself in a position in which you can intercept him on his return and take the object from him before he can reach his box, giving a tit-bit in exchange and praising him as you do so. Each time you have to remove the dummy from the puppy's mouth say DROP or GIVE quietly, being very careful not to intimidate the youngster while you open his jaws.

If you are dealing with a very recalcitrant animal, which persists in running off after he has picked up the object and refuses to bring it to you despite all your calling and coaxing, you may have recourse to a long line or cord, several yards in length. Fasten one end to the dog's collar and hold the other in your hand, leaving the rest lying loose on the ground. Throw the dummy and when it is picked up call the dog immediately. If he dashes off check his flight with the cord. Call him at once and encourage him by gestures to come to you. If he does not, pull him in steadily, all the time calling him and trying to coax him towards you. When he eventually reaches you, praise and reward him in the same way as if he had returned of his own accord. Repeat this consistently and soon you will find that only a slight jerk on the cord will be necessary to induce the dog to return, and in time he will come spontaneously. How long it will be before the line can be wholly dispensed with will depend on the intelligence and temperament of the dog concerned and with the strength of his attachment to you, but go on using the check cord until the dog can be relied on to return without fail.

As a dog becomes proficient, throw the object further and further and start practising in conditions in which the object may fall where it is not easily seen – behind a bush, in long grass, etc. If the dummy used is kept specifically for that purpose, as it should be, the dog will probably follow the direction of the throw by sight and on nearing the spot where it has fallen will actually locate it by catching its scent. After a time throw the object in cover where it is more completely hidden and, if the dog is baffled, encourage him to nose about in search of it by using such words as FIND or HI LOST! From this you may pass on to teaching him to search out an object dropped by you in cover without being thrown. A dog which has been properly trained to fetch or retrieve an object which he has seen thrown, though it is hidden from sight after it falls, will soon learn to seek out something bearing a familiar scent, like his owner's glove, purse or handkerchief, which has been left in cover while his attention is engaged elsewhere.

A dog which has learnt to fetch and bring may be taught to deliver the object in a sitting position. This may be done by uttering the command SIT as he comes up and before taking the object from him. If he has already been trained to sit on command, no difficulty should be experienced. Be sure to make a special fuss of him when he remains sitting while you take the dummy and never accept an object which he has brought without first making him sit. Never make the mistake of extending the hand for the object as the dog approaches. Keep the hands at the sides until he is close up and has obeyed the command to sit. If the dog jumps against you in his eagerness to deliver the object, press him back on the ground with an admonitory NO, followed by the command SIT.

In his enthusiasm for the game a dog may sometimes become too rampageous; jumping up and barking excitedly in anticipation of the object being thrown. To avoid this, once preliminary training in fetching has been given, you may go on to teach him that he is not to run to retrieve a thrown article until he is told. Before making a throw put the dog on the lead and give the command SIT – STAY. When he sits for a few seconds after the throw without struggling, give the command FETCH, setting him free at the same time. Reward him well on his return and repeat the lesson. Be careful not to keep the dog sitting for more than a short space each time, releasing him to fetch as soon as he sits without having to be restrained. You can, if you prefer, combat the antics of an over-exuberant dog eager for you to throw something for him to fetch, by saying NO sharply and then getting him to sit, refraining from throwing until he has obeyed. But in most cases the former method will prove the more satisfactory.

You may have to cope with a dog which, having bounded gleefully after an article and brought it back, drops it either at your feet or before he reaches you. In such circumstances pick up the object and get the dog to take it in his mouth again by putting it in and saying HOLD. If necessary, at first keep your hand round his muzzle to prevent the object being dropped again at once. When he is holding it securely, take it from him with the word GIVE. Repeat this whenever he drops the article before you can take it, rewarding him when he delivers to hand but never before.

To teach a dog to carry a basket, newspaper or other article for a more or less indefinite period and to give them up only to his owner, the first step is to make the dog realise the significance of the word Hold. If he has been trained to fetch and bring a thrown or hidden object, training will be simple. All that is needed is to make him understand that the object must be retained in the mouth until he is told to GIVE, and must be carried safely and carefully from place to place and not under any circumstances be relinquished or dropped until taken by his owner. To start with, put the dog on the lead, get him to take the object in his mouth and give the command HOLD or CARRY. Walk along with him and if he keeps the article without dropping it for a little way praise him. Should he drop it, put it again into his mouth with a sharply uttered HOLD and again move off.

Do not make the walk very long at first but gradually increase the distance. Later practise the exercise in a road where there is traffic and pedestrians. When the dog is reliable while held on the lead, let him go loose and carry a basket or similar article while walking to heel. Most dogs enjoy carrying things in their mouths and if praised and told they are 'clever' while doing so will very quickly become enthusiastic adepts.

# CHAPTER NINE

# SEEKING, SCENTING AND TRACKING

A DOG which has been taught to fetch or retrieve an article which falls in a spot in which it is not immediately visible, may later be trained to track an object by exercising his powers of scent. A dog's sense of smell is very much keener and more selective than our own. Indeed, he relies much more on this sense in identifying people, places and things than on sight. In training him to follow a trail we are, therefore, only encouraging him to make use of an inherent faculty for a particular purpose. When your dog finds a dummy which has fallen in cover he does so largely by scent. We now have to teach him to find something which he cannot see, not by searching a small area until he is guided to it by catching a whiff of its scent, but by following the trail of the person who hid it.

If you can enlist the assistance of a friend your dog's first lesson in following a trail may take the form of a game of hide and seek. Put the dog on the lead and let him be held by your assistant while you walk away. Attract his attention as you go and when some distance off slip behind a tree or building. After a pre-arranged interval, beginning with a minute or so, the assistant should let him go forward to find you, still holding him on the lead. Repeat this several times, then, after you have hidden, move further away under cover, halting in a place well out of sight of the dog some distance from where you first disappeared. When the dog reaches the spot where he lost sight of you he will have to rely on his nose to find your new position, tracking you by the scent you have left on the ground. Continue practising in this way, steadily increasing the distance and gradually making the task of finding you more difficult. Reward the dog each time he comes up to you and when he is working satisfactorily on the lead arrange with your assistant to let him loose after you have been away a certain length of time.

Begin the next phase of training by making your dog sit, show him the object to be found and let him smell it. Give the command STAY and walk somewhere out of sight and place the article on the ground. Let the dog see the direction you take as you go away, scrape your feet or well trample the ground on the spot from which you start, and walk slowly with dragging steps. This will ensure that you leave a good scent. Having disposed of the article, return to the dog, treading as nearly as possible along the same line as that traversed when going away. Stroke the dog and let him smell your hands to get your scent. Put on the lead and, pointing to the ground, say SEEK. His first impulse will probably be to pull strongly in the direction which he saw you take, in the knowledge, gained from past experience, that the article to be found will be close to where he lost sight of you. But restrain him, and by pointing repeatedly to your starting point, on which you scraped your feet to intensify the scent, bid him SEEK. He will soon find your scent and move forwards. As he does so try to get him to follow the path taken by you, encouraging him to keep his nose down by repeating SEEK, SEEK. If he lifts his head and seems to want to run forwards, direct to where he thinks the object has been hidden, stop, again point to the ground and try to get him back on the trail. When he eventually finds the object praise him heartily. Continue this lesson until your dog shows clearly that he understands that the easiest way to find what you have hidden is by following your track by scent. Later increase the length of your track, move to another place and practise on different types of ground – grass, bare soil, a path, woodland, etc.

Always leave a strong patch of scent on the spot from which

you start and as the distance covered by the track increases scrape your feet where the trail ends, so that the dog is certain to be guided to the article he is seeking at the end of his task. Always remember exactly where you hid the object and see that the dog invariably finds it. It is most important when teaching any form of tracking to ensure that a track ends with the dog being successful in coming on what he is searching for. If he fails to find after working out a scent on a trail he may lose interest and enthusiasm for what he may feel is a pointless and unrewarding game.

When your dog reaches the end of a trail, encourage him to pick up the found object, carry it back to where you started from, sit and hold it until you take it from him. Praise or reward him with a tit-bit when you relieve him of the article. When your dog has learnt this exercise thoroughly on the lead, practise him while loose. At first it is better to follow him as he tracks, so that you may correct or help him should that be required, but later put him on the track of something you have hidden unknown to him and leave him to his own devices. Remain at the starting point so that he may bring the object back to you. Once he has been trained in this way a dog may be kept in practice by quietly dropping an article carrying your scent – a glove, purse or anything else which has been worn or used constantly – during a walk then, when a suitable distance has been covered, sending him back to find it by saying SEEK; letting him smell your hand and pointing to the ground over which you have passed. If training has been satisfactory the dog should bring back the dropped object at speed and deliver it to you at the Sit. Though the primary purpose of this training is to increase control and under-standing between an owner and his dog, it may on occasions be of practical value. Thus, if in the course of a walk or ramble you should accidentally drop or leave behind a piece of personal property, it is very useful to be able to send your dog back over your track to find and retrieve the missing article.

It should be realised that the older a trail the less scent it will hold and the more difficult it will be for a dog to follow. Some kinds of ground hold scent much better than others. Atmospheric conditions may be favourable or unfavourable. For example, grass and woodland are better for scent than is dry sand or a pavement, and a dog which fails to make out a trail in dry conditions at midday may follow it quite well in the early morning or evening when the earth is slightly moist. Then, some dogs have a much keener sense of smell than others and, since success in tracking depends to a very large extent on an animal's natural faculty, it is useless to try to make a dog which has a poor nose learn to follow a trail well or with enthusiasm. It is senseless to punish a dog for failing in this kind of work. It is like punishing a deaf child for failing to hear what is said to him. If, therefore, your dog shows no aptitude for tracking, don't persist in efforts to make him. A great deal of enjoyment and interest may be obtained from the possession of a clever and well-trained tracker, but the first prerequisite for success is a dog which really enjoys tracking.

When your dog can be relied on to find and bring back an object that has been surreptitiously hidden, his scenting ability may be tested by teaching him to pick out an article bearing your scent from a number of others which you have not touched. Have the dog in a sitting position, command him to STAY and go off with the article in your hand. When out of sight place it on the ground near to several other objects which you have not handled. These may be carried on a tray of some kind or held in a pair of tongs, or placed by an assistant in the spot selected beforehand. Return to your dog and tell him to SEEK in the usual way. If he picks up the object bearing your scent praise him. But if he attempts to go to one of the others say NO sharply and direct his attention to the right one. Immediately he picks it up praise him well. Repeat this several times and soon you will find that your dog will pick out the right article every time without faltering. At first the articles used should be varied in shape, size and texture and be placed in a comparatively small area. Later scatter them more widely, alter their position in relation to one another and make them more similar in appearance. Then try mixing up a number of articles looking almost identical with yours and place them quite close together. From time to time change the object carrying your scent, so as to ensure that your dog is relying solely on his nose in discriminating between the one he is to bring and the others. A dog which has been trained to find an object by scent will very soon master this exercise. It is a very useful one to practise, as it serves to intensify a dog's association of his owner with anything which bears his scent and implants in his mind the feeling that any article which carries that scent belongs to his owner. This makes him more reliable in finding and bringing in anything that may be lost or mislaid.

Tracking proper may be considered to be an extension of the training dealt with under the heading of seeking by scent for a hidden object. In that exercise the dog is led to the article by the trail left by the person who hides it. In what may be termed serious tracking, a dog is required to follow a line of scent left on the ground by the feet of the person being tracked, whether this track was laid a few minutes or many hours before. It is, of course, much easier for a dog to track his owner whose scent is familiar than to follow the trail of a stranger.

Leave your dog behind or in charge of an assistant while you go off to lay a trail. Scrape your feet on the ground or walk about in a small circle to impregnate the starting point with your scent. Then move away, stepping heavily or dragging the feet slightly so that you leave a good strong scent behind you. When you have been gone for five minutes or so your assistant should take the dog on a lead to your starting point and hold a handkerchief, or something which you have used or carried and which, therefore, bears your scent, to the dog's nose and encourage him to sniff it. He should then be told to SEEK. His previous training should have taught him that to find you he must follow your scent, which he will pick up first from the handkerchief and then from the ground on which you have scraped your feet. He should, therefore, go forwards with his nose down and try to work out the line you have taken.

Begin by limiting the trail to a distance of about fifty yards. Gradually extend this and increase the interval between laying the trail and putting the dog on. In the early stages make the track over unfrequented ground, so that your scent will not be crossed by that of strangers, but when the dog has had some practice he may be asked to follow a trail over country where it is likely to be crossed and re-crossed several times by other walkers and animals.

The purpose of teaching a dog to track its owner is to accustom him to picking up a scent from an object held to his nose. When he understands that he is to follow any track carrying the same scent as that borne by an object presented to him to sniff while being told to SEEK, he will soon learn to track a stranger as readily as he will follow the trail of his owner. Though it is, perhaps, unlikely that the ordinary owner of a pet or companion dog will wish to undertake training in advanced tracking, the elements of such training may be satisfactorily inculcated in the manner indicated. For further and more detailed instruction an experienced and qualified expert should be consulted.

# CHAPTER TEN

# CHASING TRAFFIC AND FARM STOCK

A TENDENCY to bark at or run after bicycles or cars, or to chase poultry, sheep, cattle or other farm stock, must be checked immediately it shows itself. Once this habit is formed a dog becomes a liability to its owner, whom it may involve in heavy damages, besides being a menace to road users, farmers and domestic animals. In addition the dog runs grave risks of being killed or badly injured whenever it is loose, or may meet a premature end by being shot or ordered to be destroyed.

Bicycle chasing or barking at traffic should not occur if a puppy is taught traffic sense from the time it is first taken out on a lead. As soon as he has learnt to go well on the lead, take the youngster along a road where there is a good deal of traffic. Some puppies may find the noise disconcerting at first and show fear or nervousness, but will soon become bolder if soothed and reassured each time they shy away from passing vehicles. In extreme cases the dog should be picked up and carried for a time while the owner continues to walk along the busy road. Talk to the puppy and when he seems less nervous put him down and coax him along, speaking quietly to him and trying to make him understand that there is nothing to be alarmed about. If this is done consistently each day any normal puppy will learn to walk fearlessly along a main road however heavy or noisy the traffic. A bolder or more assertive youngster may be excited by the bustle, and pull towards a passing vehicle, barking. Many thoughtless owners think this is amusing and shows spirit and courage. They fail to realise that by permitting a puppy to behave in this way without correcting him sharply and at once, they are encouraging the development of a habit which will probably cause a great deal of trouble later on. When a dog of any age pulls towards a passing cyclist or car check him at once by jerking the lead sharply, saying NO firmly and reprovingly. Jerk the offender back every time he misbehaves. Watch him carefully and whenever he allows a vehicle to go by without attempting to bark or pull towards it praise him. Take him along roads where there is much traffic, or where cyclists are likely to be seen, and miss no opportunity to correct any tendency to run at or after them. A dog which is inured to walking along a busy thoroughfare will soon learn to ignore traffic of all kinds and will never thereafter give any trouble when running loose.

A dog which chases poultry may be dealt with in much the same way. Keep him on a lead and take him as often as possible to places where he is likely to see poultry at close quarters. Immediately he shows any sign of wanting to run at them jerk him back sharply, saying NO loudly and clearly. Repeat this regularly until the dog makes no further attempts to get at any of the birds among which he is taken. Later, if it can be arranged, it is a good idea to tie him up in a poultry enclosure. Stay near by ready to say NO and go to him and smack him should he try to go for a hen. Then leave him again. If he remains quiet as the birds move about him praise him and reward him with a tit-bit. When he seems trustworthy on the lead let him run loose where poultry are to be seen. Correct him immediately he misbehaves, if necessary putting him on the lead again while you keep him walking among the birds.

A dog which has been trained to walk to heel on command is, of course, very much easier to teach not to chase. Any attempt to go after a cyclist or farm animal may be checked at once by calling him to heel. It is, however, necessary to make the dog understand that in giving chase he is committing an offence. This is best accomplished by having the dog on the lead even if he is walking to heel, so that any attempt to leave his position to chase may be immediately corrected by a sharp jerk of the lead and an admonishing NO. If he is merely called to heel when he shows signs of chasing he may, if properly trained, come as commanded, but this may only indicate obedience to a familiar word of command and not be associated with any prohibition of chasing as such. He may, therefore, continue to have the desire to chase in your absence or when your attention is distracted from him.

Sheep seem to have a special fascination for dogs, probably because they run away immediately they are approached and by their actions invite any normally active or boisterous dog to chase them in play. But what may represent only playfulness in a dog may have very serious consequences. It is not only the so-called killer dog which is responsible for the deaths and maiming of sheep. Some of the sheep chased in all innocence by a puppy or adult dog of a breed far too small to inflict real injury even should it catch its quarry, may be in lamb and suffer fatal damage from abortion or exhaustion as a result of a youngster's frolicsome antics.

It is vitally important that a companion dog should be trained to be absolutely safe with sheep, and the earlier this is done the better. The first lessons may be given on an ordinary lead, jerking the dog back with a stern NO when he shows the least inclination to chase. Continue this routine, taking the dog frequently across fields in which sheep are grazing, so that he gets used to seeing them and innured to the temptation they offer when they run away as you pass by. Correct every lunge in their direction with a strong jerk of the lead and the reproof NO. Go on doing this until he will walk quietly through a flock at pasture without showing undue interest in them or trying to pull towards them.

When he has reached this stage you may feel justified in trying him off the lead. That, however, is far too risky. It cannot be too strongly emphasised that the sight of running sheep seems to offer a well-nigh irresistible temptation to some dogs to chase – probably only in fun. Unfortunately, as already explained, the harmlessness of a dog's intentions has no relation to the harm the sheep may suffer through being run by him. Furthermore, a dog which begins to chase sheep without any desire to catch or injure them, may succumb to an upsurge of the primitive hunting instinct in the excitement of the chase and be guilty of savaging any sheep he is able to come up with. Instead, therefore, of letting your dog run loose among sheep after he appears to be safe while on the lead, it is wiser to replace the comparatively short lead ordinarily used by a long check cord, not heavy enough to impede his freedom of movement but strong enough to control his most furious rushes, and from ten to twenty yards in length.

Fasten this to the collar, hold the end tightly in the hand and let the slack lie on the ground. If more convenient the line may be wound on a reel from which it will run out smoothly when pulled. The main point is that the dog should be able to run ahead without being conscious of a feeling of restraint. If, on seeing a sheep, he makes a dash towards it give him a chance to get into his stride then give him a sharp and sudden jerk by means of the check cord, calling NO at the same time. Then command HERE. If he comes praise him, but if he does not draw him in by the cord. As soon as he reaches you praise him. In this way you will be correcting him for chasing but rewarding him for obeying your command to come to you. If you punish him when he comes to you there is a strong probability that he will associate your displeasure not with chasing but with returning to your call, and that is something which must be avoided at all times.

Continue to use the check cord until you are perfectly sure that your dog is really dependable when brought into contact with sheep. Do not be in too great a hurry to discard it, and do not always check the dog at the same distance. If you do he may come to regard the cord as a lead and learn nothing new from its use. With a dog which is difficult to break of chasing it is advisable to let him get some considerable way before applying the check. The reason for this is that the further a dog runs, as a rule, the faster he will be moving, and the faster he is going the more severe the jerk he will experience when arrested by the check cord.

Even when your dog is believed to be completely trained to sheep, always keep an eye on him when in the vicinity of a flock. If he comes on a bunch of sheep which suddenly start off in a panic, the temptation to go after them may be so strong as to cause him to forget his training. Always be on the alert to call him up immediately he shows the first signs of wishing to chase the fleeing company. In hilly country, where your dog is likely to be out of sight from time to time when running loose, play safe by keeping him on a lead or at least by walking him to heel where you have him under close control. The fact is, that although it is not difficult to teach a dog that sheep chasing is prohibited, it is practically impossible to be quite certain that circumstances will never arise which will tempt him to transgress despite his training, when he is running at liberty where there are sheep. You should at all times ensure that during a country walk or picnic your dog is not allowed to roam, even for a short time, beyond the limits of your absolute control.

So much is heard these days of the havoc wrought to sheep by wandering dogs that it seems advisable to emphasise that however satisfactory a dog may seem to have responded to training in making him safe with livestock, it is nevertheless very unwise to believe that he will always be similarly well-behaved in this respect when he is away from your influence. When on his own he may very quickly fall into the habit of sheep chasing. This is especially likely to happen if he goes off roaming with a canine companion. Two or more dogs together are very much more apt to get into mischief than one. Several together may revert to hunting or chasing as a pack and soon become dominated by primitive ancestral instincts which prompt them to pull down and kill anything which tries to evade capture by running.

# CHAPTER ELEVEN

# TRAINING TO WATER
# AND GUARDING

I F YOU live near a river or the sea you may wish to train your dog to swim and enjoy the water. Whether or not he is easy to train in this respect will depend on his breed and disposition. Some dogs enter the water happily and boldly even as puppies, but others are very nervous at first and unless dealt with understandingly may be terrified by their owners' efforts to make them swim. As a rule, a dog that shows a strong aversion to going into water when encouraged to do so has been frightened at some time by being dropped or thrown in against its will. The old idea that any dog can be made to swim and enjoy water by being forcibly pushed or taken in the sea or a river out of its depth, is as ill-founded as the supposition that a young bird taken from the nest will instinctively spread its wings and fly if thrown into the air. Many a dog that is water shy has been made so by such senseless treatment. The first essential is to familiarise the pupil with being in the vicinity of water and to make him realise that coming in contact with it has no unpleasant results.

The best time to start training is on a warm day, when getting wet will not be attended by an uncomfortable shock. Find a spot where the ground slopes gently down to the water or, if by the sea, when it is calm and the tide is out. Play with the dog by throwing a stick or other easily carried article which will float, and let him fetch and bring it back to you in the usual way. When he is enjoying the game, throw the object to be retrieved so that it falls at the edge of or just in the water. In his excitement the dog will probably run to ge it and in so doing get his feet wet. Repeat this several times, being careful not to make the object fall in a greater depth of water than can be reached by a little shallow paddling. Practise for a few days, and when your dog shows no hesitation in paddling to fetch the article, gradually increase the distance from the bank or shore. But do not throw so far out that your dog cannot get to it while touching the bottom with his feet. This is important, as the dog's confidence must be built up before trying to get him to go fearlessly out of his depth. Once he has become used to being in the water he will not hesitate to go for the object when it is thrown a bit further out than before; in his excitement making a few floundering strokes before turning to come back when he finds he is out of his depth.

The time taken to reach this stage of training will vary much with individual dogs, but never try to hurry matters. Let the dog itself decide when he is ready to venture into deeper water, so that there is no risk of his learning to associate being in the water with fear. Do not let your dog suffer from cold after swimming. Give him a brisk run and rub him down well as soon as he gets home or, if convenient, take a towel with you to dry him when his game in the water is finished. Do not try to make him go into rough water or through breakers until he is used to swimming.

Once he has been accustomed to going into shallow water he may be induced to swim by being played with on the bank or shore where there are other dogs running in and out of the water and swimming freely In the general excitement he will probably join them and start swimming without further encouragement. Further practice may be given by leaving him with a friend while you go to the opposite bank and then call him. Or you may go into the water yourself and when a few yards out try to persuade the dog to swim to you. At first his attempts to swim will be awkward and clumsy and he will tire quickly. Until he is a proficient swimmer and enjoys being in the water, therefore, lessons should be of short duration. Provide the dog with frequent opportunities of playing on the bank or shore between practices in the water and do everything possible to make him look forward with eager anticipation to the periods of aquatic training.

Many people who acquire a puppy soon begin to wonder what steps should be taken to make him a good guard. Often they are disappointed because for a time he shows no signs of assuming an attitude of protection towards his owner or the house which constitutes his home. The belief that the instinct to guard a certain person or his property can be brought into being by training is a mistake. Before a dog develops a feeling of responsibility to protect anyone or anything he must first become attached to them -- recognising the one as his beloved and trusted owner and the other as his personal property. At what age this feeling will develop varies greatly. As a rule, however, a dog cannot reasonably be expected to feel the protective instinct at all strongly until well out of puppyhood. In some cases it may be two years before a dog shows evidence of becoming a good guard.

Different people have very different ideas as to what is needed in a dog which they would regard as a dependable guard. So far as the ordinary companion dog is concerned, a savage animal which will growl suspiciously at every stranger who calls at the house, or attack an intruder on sight, is very far from being what is wanted. On the contrary, an animal of this kind is almost sure to be not merely a nuisance but a menace both to its owner and to everyone else who comes in contact with him. Except in special cases, a house dog is required to give warning of the approach or the presence of strangers by barking and to indicate his intention of protecting his owner and his property by assuming a threatening attitude towards a would-be assailant. Almost any dog which has formed a close attachment to his owner or home will behave in this way when occasion demands. The fact that a dog is generally inclined to be friendly with visitors or callers does not necessarily imply that he will be of little use as a guard.

If you wish to ensure that your dog becomes a good guard and decide to help towards that end by training, the first thing is to make up your mind just how you want him to behave in the presence of strangers. For example, if you expect him to give warning by barking, do not correct him by shouting QUIET whenever he barks at a strange noise or a knock at the door during the day when you are expecting a caller. By so doing you may be teaching him to refrain from barking at similar noises at any time, whether you are there or not. A better plan is to say 'ALL right, old boy', pat him and let him go to the door with you. Before opening the door get him to sit beside or slightly in front of you. See that he remains sitting in this position while you speak with the caller. Do not allow him to be fondled while in this position. If the visitor is admitted into the house let him greet the dog with friendly overtures and encourage the dog to accept them. In this way your dog will always be in a position to protect you from a strange caller with evil intentions, towards whom an attitude of suspicion may be maintained, but will soon understand that a person brought into the house by you is to be treated as a friend. A dog which is too boisterous and apt to get out of control when a caller knocks, should be taken to the door on a lead and made to sit before the door is opened. If he tries to get to the caller or barks for no reason give a sharp jerk with the lead and say QUIET. Always have him between you and the caller, keep him sitting and, if the visitor is asked in, ask him to speak to or stroke the dog, to establish friendly relations, without exciting him unduly.

A dog which is unreasonably suspicious or unfriendly towards all strangers, may be made more sociable by being taken about among people and introduced and spoken to by those he does not know. Suspicion or standoffishness is often a symptom of a nervous temperament, which may be overcome by making the animal realise that all unknown persons are not to be regarded as enemies. On the other hand, a young dog may be too eager to accept everyone as a friend and remain quite indifferent to the approach of a stranger or a knock on the door. The dog will probably grow out of this too-complaisant attitude, but meanwhile the urge to bark may be encouraged by his owner saying in an excited tone 'What's that?' when a knock is heard. Take him to the door with you and be sure to praise him when he barks either in response to your words 'What's that?' when first uttered or when they are repeated before you open the door.

As already mentioned, the great majority of dogs will give warning of danger or endeavour to protect their owners in an emergency without special training, provided they have formed a real attachment to them. It is a great and dangerous mistake for the ordinary owner to try to train his dog to attack another person on command. The only result such inexpert training is likely to have is to make the dog vicious and unreliable. Such a dog is almost invariably very difficult to handle or control except by a qualified trainer of long experience, and is quite unsuitable for life as a family companion. However good a guard may be he should always be under complete control. He should never get out of hand, come immediately he is called, under all circumstances, and obey all commands without hesitation, even in conditions of great excitement. Remember that all training in guard duties, even the simplest, must be regulated according to the temperament and the size or the strength of the animal being trained. There is no reason whatever why a thoroughly reliable guard dog should not also be a happy, pleasant and friendly companion

CHAPTER TWELVE

## *SOME FINAL REMINDERS*
## *AND HINTS*

WHEN TRAINING your dog never lose your temper. If he persistently misbehaves or fails to do as he is told, try to find out why. It is probably because your training is at fault, or he may not understand what you want him to do. It is safe to assume that he is not being wilfully disobedient.

Kindness and common sense are essential qualities in anyone who wishes to succeed as a trainer. There must also be affection for, and sympathy with, the animal to be trained, as well as almost inexhaustable patience.

To teach your dog anything satisfactorily you must start with a clear idea of what you want him to learn. Don't teach a puppy a mode of behaviour which you may later consider undesirable. Remember that a trick which may be amusing in a small puppy may be very unfunny in a full grown dog.

As training proceeds you may find that your dog likes to perform certain exercises but obviously dislikes doing others. To keep him good tempered and amenable spend only short periods practising the latter but much longer on the others. Be very generous in praising or rewarding him when he carries out, or tries to carry out, a command which he finds disagreeable. If you are careful not to irritate him or rouse his resentment by too frequent repetition, he will probably lose his initial prejudice in time and eventually go through the exercises happily and enthusiastically.

Always watch your dog's reactions to each lesson. Make a point of bringing a session to a close as soon as he has made some effort to act in the way you desire, immediately he shows signs of being bored or fatigued, or looks worried and unhappy.

All training methods are based ultimately on the judicious application of correction and reward. Never miss an opportunity of rewarding your dog when he does, or tries to do, as commanded, or of correcting him when he fails to do so. When you have occasion to correct or punish do it at once, so that your dog associates your displeasure or the discomfort you cause him with the act for which you are correcting him. Make all correction sharp· and clear and when you have inflicted a correction resume friendly relations at once. Don't grumble or nag at a dog, and never reprove him for something he did some time ago and which he has forgotten; as he cannot possibly associate being admonished or punished with the offence you condemn.

Remember that the tone of voice in which you speak to your dog will probably convey more to him than the actual words you use. A scared or timid dog may be soothed and quietened by being talked to gently and with confidence.

If your dog runs away in a panic, never chase or shout at him. That will only increase his fear. Call him by name and do everything possible by encouraging words and actions to persuade him to approach you, and be sure to reward him immediately he comes.

Ideally, training should be approached by both trainer and dog as a game to be shared and enjoyed. But make sure that the game never gets beyond your control. Make your dog understand that though you are his very special friend you are also the boss. Try to make every lesson pleasant, interesting and enjoyable. This will ensure that your dog not only obeys your commands but that he does so unhesitatingly and willingly.

You cannot expect any success in training unless you win your dog's affection and trust. Never underestimate the importance of retaining his confidence, not only in yourself but in other members of the family, in all kinds of surroundings in and out of doors. This is the best way to ensure that he grows up bold and fearless, with a feeling of friendliness for all with whom he is brought in contact. There is no reason why a dog should be bad tempered, unreliable, nervous or suspicious if he is taught from puppyhood to regard humans, whether adults or children, as friends.

With few exceptions a dog is never untrainable at any age; in the sense that he may be broken of bad habits and made safe, obedient and subject to proper control wherever he may be. With skill and patience any dog can be made responsive to training. But it is much easier and quicker to train a puppy than an older dog. A puppy matures much more quickly than a child and at six or nine months may be quite ready to be put into serious training. Remember, however, that training methods must be flexible and correction must always be varied to suit the age, size and disposition of the individual dog being dealt with.

Throughout training make it your constant endeavour to establish a bond of confidence and faith between yourself and your dog. Never break faith with him nor abuse his trust.

When playing with a puppy never let the game involve teasing or inciting him to struggle to keep what he is holding or to wrest something from you. If he seems to be getting too boisterous or excited stop the game before you lose control. Rough play in puppyhood is almost sure to lead to trouble as the dog grows up.

If you have a full grown dog which has become aggressive towards people or other dogs, or has other bad habits which you feel it is beyond you to correct, take him to a training class to be dealt with by an experienced trainer. Wherever you live there is almost sure to be a training class held within easy reach. If in doubt write to the Secretary of the Kennel Club, 1-4 Clarges Street, Piccadilly, London, W.1, enclosing a stamped addressed envelope, asking for the address of the training centre nearest your home.

# INDEX

# INDEX